M000273389

Burst & Fleurish

MICHELLE J. KAPLAN

ISBN 978-1-09831-398-2 eBook 978-1-09831-399-9

Cover art by Mitch Rosacker
Book cover design by Suzanne Verba-Hopkins
Author's headshot taken by Michelle Arpin Begina

Praise For *Burst & Fleurish*

If you are ready to "burst" into a new and wondrous life, read this book of poetry cover to cover. Inspiring, deeply reflective and yet accessible, Michelle is the poet for the female heart. The message she shares is medicine for the soul, providing hope that we too can find our true life's purpose and revel in the feminine emotions that are truly our gift. Michelle has such high hopes for humanity; that we will find the best part of ourselves, that we will reach out to each other with love and compassion, that we will *be love with all in every*. This book will transform you, will motivate you to be more, do more, and feel more. Thank you Michelle, for allowing us into your heart, and for loving us in all of our frailty and beautiful messiness.

~ Tresa Leftenant, Founder, Reinventing Her Money Guiding Professional Women to Live a Wealthy Life on Her Terms

Michelle captures life in words to describe our rich inner experience of how the outside world touches us.

~ Michelle Arpin Begina, Founder & Gateway of MichelleAB

Now more than ever humanity needs its focus on beauty, truth, laughter, and love. Michelle Kaplan's new book, *Burst & Fleurish*, gifts readers with all four. Skillfully and thoughtfully written and deeply personal, this book is a moving example of the power of words and the art of poetry. A delightful read in every way!

~ Louis Efron, Globally recognized writer, speaker, and award-winning Fortune 200 people executive

Burst & Fleurish is a thought-provoking follow-up to *and: A love story within*. Uniquely Michelle, the poems capture the essence we can all identify with as we navigate the frustration and chaos of our lives in search of our true selves. Michelle writes of experiences personal and universal as well as those simple and profound. Her voice is quiet and comforting and her style measured and approachable. She listens with her heart and sees with her soul. From wistful recollections of childhood, to poignant reflections on motherhood, to the hell of battling a life-threatening disease, Michelle is the voice of unwavering honesty. Michelle invites us to tag along on her quest for her essential self and along the way encourages all of us to seek our own.

~ Dennis Leogrande, The Great Kate Studio

Michelle Kaplan has written a beautiful book of poetry, bringing her deep and meaningful thoughts (musings) to many of the challenges we all face. Michelle's poems always inspire me to open myself up to the vulnerabilities and uncertainties, but also the wonder and hope of life as I progress on my own path. There is a raw authenticity to what is presented here that seems in striking contrast to our overly orchestrated world. Looking deep into one's Self (soul) can at times be painful, but Michelle invites us all in to comfortably allow for that exploration.

~ Lauren Myler, LCSW, OSW-C, Therapist in Private Practice

Michelle Kaplan's second collection of poems, *Burst & Fleurish*, thoughtfully blends honesty, vulnerability and love into the most delicious treat for the soul! Taking this introspective journey with her is just what we need to embrace our own hidden truths and find our courage. Thank you, Michelle, for sharing your gift with us.

~ Joyce Fein, Founder, Building Confidence! For Single Working Moms over 45

We all need things of beauty in our lives.
A beautiful book of poetry ... *Burst & Fleurish*
An author sharing her inner beauty ... Michelle Kaplan
And ... *Beautiful* ...
I think I'll go with *that* today.

~ Rosemarie M.

Michelle Kaplan has a way of finding wonder in the everyday and joy in looking deep within herself. She reminds us of what it means to be human, that inner voice that's with us our entire lives, that sense of wonder, memory and dreaming all while being grounded in reality. Michelle soars and takes us along on her journey of pain, release, and joy.

~ Maureen Buscareno, Founder of Moon Over the Trees Music and Theatre Productions

CONTENTS

PART 2: BURST

The Heart Raptured

A Perspective Textured

PART 3: FLEURISH

A New Journey Ventured

A Life Nonforfeitured

THE INVITATION

In Their Shoes

Imagine, if you will,
all that they've been
born into,
taught,
witnessed,
and experienced
that made them
who they are today.

Can you envision
what the world
would be like
if you walked
in their shoes
and they walked
in yours?

A universe,
stepping in time
to the souls
of love.

PREFACE

The cluttered mind was now evidenced on the freshly written pages of my journal. A verbal regurgitation of my worries and fears that didn't bring me the clarity I was seeking. Then, out of nowhere, a word captured my attention, a simple phrase sung in my heart, and a poem was coded like a download onto a computer. And it eased my pain and gave me hope. So I did it again... and again... and again.

Poetry is the experience of us. A storyteller of our hearts and imaginations that is wonderfully personal and curiously universal. Poetry...subtle, elusive, nonlinear, and unrestrained, warmly greets you at the door, providing what you need, giving what you're open to receiving. There is nothing to analyze, no one right way to understand since poetry transports us out of our minds and into that intuitive dwelling within all of us that just knows. It's that place that brings us a pure and unseasoned perspective, filled with vitality and compassion, on the old and worn.

Poetry, a vehicle to self-discovery, offers us the space to experience vulnerability and humility, an openness and strength not seen every day in this coping-addicted, plastic world that's uncommonly intriguing. Behind the masks we wear in our daily masquerade, we recognize ourselves in its offerings we call poems and creates a sense of belonging and healing. Through someone else's story, we get a greater sense of our own. A few words, arranged in a certain order, can change the world.

Our world. Your world. A world where, more than ever, we need to pull together, not push apart. It really is quite simple in the end. After all the drama and angst, it turns out that the bottom line is…there is none. And Truth is an open vastness going nowhere in particular other than in the direction of love. But all the layers of mud you traipsed through are not fraught with naught. As you dig and clear down to the roots of you, the landscape changes from scarcity to abundance when you change your perspective from fear to love. And then everything changes in and around us, the world seen more like the view from a kaleidoscope than a telescope so we can burst forth and live a life that's flourishing.

As I continued writing, *Burst & Fleurish* emerged, becoming the unintended and inevitable sequel to my first book *and: A love story within*. To burst and fleurish is the process of getting out of your head and more into that intuitive dwelling that resides within you, that's been there all along, accessing the place that does know the answer and sometimes changes the questions, shifting your perspective to more compassion and understanding with the relationship with yourself and others, feeling more connected to your surroundings, now more kinder and gentler, being able to receive, not just give abundance and acceptance so you feel like you belong, which allows easier access to your core genius creativity so you can contribute and make a difference in this crazy world.

Poetry is contemporary, relevant, and cool because it's the language of dream makers, journey takers, rule breakers, business shakers, soul wakers, and freedom stakers. Come dream with me to a new reality...

With love and gratitude,
Michelle
May 1, 2020

PROLOGUE

Sending Love

Love defines all meaning.
Love defies all loss.

My Legacy

To those I've loved…
I hope you laugh out loud
at how loud I was,
and how I liked everything
put away and in its place
before going to bed,
in the hopes
of gaining some semblance
of control
I never really felt in life,
and how impatient I was
when someone
was taking longer
than I thought they should have
in pretty much anything,
and how much I hated those
self service registers at stores
that are gaining in popularity,
not because I was above
checking out my purchases,
but that it only deepened
the disconnectedness I felt,
empty in a store
full of people,
and how I swore more
than I should have,
not to be disrespectful or crude,
but out of the Eureka
of finding the perfect word
that sometimes matched
the goings-on in this bleepin' world,

and who felt things
much too deeply
for even you
to understand,
and who sometimes reacted
from my wounded self
when I wanted to be
all zen and chill,
and who kept secrets
to protect you
more than me,
and who carried the weight
of feeling like
I never had enough
time, money, or energy
to spend on you,
and the guilt trips I took
of all the trips
we didn't take together,
and man, oh, the fun we did have
with the ones that were taken,
and how not easy it was
to give up ice cream, milk chocolate,
and my other favorite foods,
but I did,
not because I'm disciplined
or trying to be flawless,
but in exchange
for feeling better,
so I could be better
for you,
and how annoying I was
in the mornings,

running, talking, writing,
full of energy,
being a big tidal wave
when all you wanted
was a still, quiet lake,
and how I changed my mind
when you least expected me to
and remained optimistically stubborn
when you needed some slack.

So no regrets or do overs
in the mind.
You know I loved you
more than my shoes,
and promise me,
yes…promise,
you'll remember me
this way,
a simple contradiction,
a living oxymoron,
and not as a saint,
because that's not true,
and memorializing me
as something I wasn't
negates what I
was continually striving for
in life.

Truth.

So laugh and cry
at our memories,
but mostly laugh
at the celebration

of all of me,
an imperfect person
who tried her best,
for the best,
and failed.
Except with you,
the ones I leave behind,
nothing could be further
from the truth.

After

The safety
of her sheltered world
shattered,
she grieves her loss,
seizing what's lost,
her stolen dreams
washed away
through the raw abandon
of dirty tears.

Alive,
but dead inside,
a resistance existence,
her heart sheetrocked,
walled off from her
insufferable emotions,
the pain,
too much to bear.

But out and around
the numbing of her
self-protected confinement,
her soul still burns
and yearns
to feel again,
even that,
because it can survive,
she can survive,
anything.

This is what happens…
before.

PART 1: BEFORE

Filleted

I want to change
without being changed.
That's like changing
your reflection in the mirror
with a new mirror.

The Body Fractured

Midnight Snack

Are your cravings
feeding your fears
or your soul?

Portion Size

Do I relish
each morsel of you
or do I starve myself
in the hopes
of receiving the whole dish,
knowing I could go hungry
forever?
I really don't have an appetite
for hunger games
and I don't want to leave
a bad aftertaste.
I just understand
we're all made of pure, organic ingredients,
injected with artificial fillers and flavors,
after having been grown
from processed food for thoughts.
So I'll keep savoring each taste,
awaiting to serve and be served
the bitter and the sweet.
It's all complicatedly delicious.

Hunger Pains

She has the worst case
of spring fever,
baring her soul
instead of her body,
not summer ready.

No, you're not lazy,
undisciplined, and
you haven't given up.
It's just your way of coping.
I get it.

Deprivation and binging
are fed by the taste of lack,
but who we really are
is savory, full, and enough.
Once you bite into that
you'll realize
you were always beautiful
and weightless.

Unchained

I gave up on myself
gradually,
unconsciously,
by numbing the senses
with things
that caused me
to block out All
because I didn't want to feel It,
until I grew
and knew,
that doesn't work
either,
anymore.
So I sat in the uneasiness
of a place
between here and there,
until the day
I stopped, started, and changed
for no better reason
than I didn't want
to feel like crap,
at my own doing,
ever again.

Beautiful

Looking back,
it was the girls
who made me feel
unpretty
and the boys and I
who believed them.

And now,
looking at my reflection
in the mirror
brings it all back.

Time isn't forgiving
to the body and mind,
but to my soul,
I was, am, and will always
be beautiful.
I think I'll go with *that* today.

Mindful Consumption

I was totally justified
in eating it,
drinking it,
buying it,
but lately, my insides
haven't been matching my out,
and I had too much
to do the next day
to feel lousy
after a moment
of imitation gratification.
I didn't give in
because there wasn't
anything to give up.
Just simply giving.

Bed Rest

There's something comforting
about giving in,
focusing complete awareness
on feeling better and getting well,
my form being overly dramatic,
knowing it's the only way
to get my attention
to slow down these days.
And now, with my nose
the only thing running,
I've surrendered by hunkering down,
letting my body work
on the undetectable
and my soul on the unseen
to allow my mind to rest finally,
accepting that whatever didn't get done today
will have to wait for tomorrow.

My Own Care Giver

I glance around
at all the pairs
waiting to be seen too.
I hear the reassuring words,
see the holding of hands,
the rubbing of one's back,
strikingly simple gestures
of caring.

I sit in the same doctor's
waiting room,
by myself,
flipping through a magazine,
legs crossed,
taking it all in.
If you can't hang with me
through the difficult
then you sure
can't have a ticket
for the easy.

Misdiagnosis

For years, I've been asking you
to scratch the surface,
but you were steadfast
in your tunnel vision
that revealed everything was normal
when it really wasn't.

And I knew that too.
I just didn't know what to call it,
but it wasn't a hypochondriac,
just a person searching for the name
to these feelings.

But no, I'm not mad at you.
You were trying to save the world,
and in the process,
didn't see the one
sitting across from you
in the other chair
who could help you do
just that.

Scarred

What were once
cuts and bruises
are now scars,
inside and out
that I don't share
with everyone
because there is such a thing
as too much information.
Yet, not showing my scars
to anyone
isn't good either.
But if I show you my scars,
they may make you
run or hide
because they aren't pretty or easy.
I'm not looking for you to remove them.
Just to see them as they are,
a badge of courage,
the marks of a survivor.

Hair Today, Gone Tomorrow

Offering me
her hair stylist's name and number,
unsolicited,
and out of place,
though well intentioned,
left me questioning.

I mean, I've always had
a love-hate relationship
with my hair.
I can recall
when a picture was taken
based on my attempts at
Dorothy Hamill's short and sassy cut,
to Farrah's feathers, and big 80's hair.
And after all the perms, bobs, and frosting,
I finally came to terms with my locks...
when I suddenly lost it all,
insult on injury,
from cancer treatments.

I don't know how to explain
the feeling
of being in the shower
with fistful clumps of hair
coming off your head
by the mere touch of water,
only to then experience,
when you get out,
your reflection in the mirror,
patches of bald spots between tufts of hair.
There is no more hiding out

from what's happening.
And though I could have worn a wig,
I chose not to
mainly because it felt so freeing,
to walk around unapologetically
as who I am right now,
my way of trying to accept
the situation thrust upon me.

Hair is the ultimate accessory,
communicating who we are.
It's why so many of us
grow our hair out
when we get married,
and cut it short when we get divorced,
and why we revere our hair stylists,
who serve as our
"bartenders", miracle workers, and cheerleaders.

Hair, a symbol of strength and beauty
like Samson or Rapunzel,
can make us feel like less
when we have less,
but what I've come to know
through the years
is that if we remember who we truly are,
it all becomes rather insignificant after all.

So though my hair grew back
finer, straighter, and grayer,
causing more bad hair days than not,
I sit here now,
writing in the early morning,
with a massive case of bedhead…
grateful for second chances.

Body Betrayal

When your body betrays you,
again and again,
you feel like
there's nowhere to turn,
so sick and tired
of being
sick and tired.

When your body betrays you,
you feel attacked
on a whole other level,
a personal invasion,
a civil war,
where there are no winners.

And though your body betrayed you,
you never betrayed yourself
because you're the one
who never gave up,
advocating to be heard, seen, and validated
for knowing your own body enough
to discern there's something bigger
going on here,
even if you don't know exactly
what that is yet.

Betraying yourself
would have come
at the ultimate cost,
and you never did
and never will.

Sustenance

Running in the rain,
all alone
in the dark,
the warmth of my blood
pulses through me
while the cold raindrops
pelt my face,
listening to my chosen song
and inner melody,
feeling strong
and small,
seeing the unseen,
peace amidst the storm.
It's the fragrance
of these times
I'll miss the most
when I'm gone.

The Mind Captured

Hoarse

I keep calling out for her,
her name caught
in my cupped hands
around my chapped lips,
but the undying winds
keeps carrying my voice away,
unheard.

Acceptance will come
when forgiveness remains.

Do You Know Where Your Children Are?

We tell our kids
how we kept the doors unlocked,
and played outside
without a grownup around,
and rode our bikes
all over town
for like, forever,
until the glow
from the streetlights
or our Moms,
yelling our names,
told us to come home,
and how we walked
right into amusement parks and concerts
with just our tickets and spending money,
without metal detectors
and bag checkers,
and how our phone calls
were also monitored
as we pulled the cord
from the kitchen phone
as far away from any eavesdroppers
in the den,
and how our questionable behavior
was recorded by our neighbor's
with the threat of telling our parents,
and the biggest scare
and annoyance
was having to wait
to eat our Halloween candy
until our parents checked

for razor blades
oh, and that we wore
flammable pajamas to bed,
and war was a thing
that you read about in history books
and saw happening in distant lands,
far, far away
on the six o'clock news,
and though our childhood wasn't
idyllic or quintessential by any means,
we tell our kids how we kept the doors unlocked.

I wonder what our kids
will tell theirs...

Unfun

I think I forgot
how to have fun.
You know, the old-fashioned kind,
joy that stuck on you like glue.
I used to be able
to make anything fun,
but now, the cloak of responsibility
hangs on me like a wet rag,
making everything feel heavy and hard.

I want to feel light again.

Squalls

They come in fast and furious,
this flurry of icy emotions,
carried by gusts of grief
that fly in and around my head,
causing whiteout conditions
where I can't see clearly.

And just like that,
the storm is over,
yet I'm left raw,
shivering.
Deep winter is upon us
with no signs of spring.

Edgeless Edginess

I lay there,
so tired,
yet feel the restlessness
course through my body,
this ball of energy,
one part inspiration,
the other angst,
the push and pull
of closing the gap
from here to there,
searching for what
we're all seeking.

The Game of Life

You keep playing
the blame game,
while I continue
the shame game,
but really,
it's all the same,
regardless of its name
and your desired aim,
I'm not your opponent
and there are no winners,
so you can cheat
if you want to,
but your next move
is the prize you claim.

Shaken

What's the balance
between accepting what is
and wanting something more?
How can I remain unattached
to what's vital to my existence?
Is that even true,
is anything completely vital to my existence?
Who am I really
if I prefer to live in the clouds
without stable footing on the ground?
Am I making things worse
by going after what will benefit many,
living precariously, even for my liking,
when I'm the only one who can see it
for now,
with no assurances that it will even happen?

The questions of a dreamer
shaken to the core.

De-Fence Less

Fences are put up
to keep some in
and others out.
Knocking down fences
because we're fenced off
is more than just for show.
Even a white picket one
separates.

Putting It to Rest

On the cusp of asleepness,
when the deep seed of fear
takes root
and comes out of hiding
from the heavy, dark vessel
it was shoved into,
which in the dawn
seems so innocuous and unassuming,
me being silly and overdramatic,
until night falls
once again.

Civil War

They were just going to work,
a painfully ordinary day,
living the American dream
believing the lie
until the end.
They never did get home that night,
their abandoned cars
proof of their disappearance
from this Earth.
It was hard enough
that it happened to us
from outsiders,
but the war isn't over.
It's just turned
to us versus us.

When we spin insiders
into outsiders,
the circle of us
keeps getting smaller and smaller.

A civil war is beginning.
A civil war is our ending.

Carry On

The sweetest betrayal
at the hands
of the most unlikely suspect,
makes me applaud
your achievement
and the enormity
of your lack
because I don't even think
you completely comprehend
the impact of you,
like a feather
floating on the uneven gusts of wind,
never finding a place to rest.
The sweetest betrayal
at the hands
of the most unlikely suspect,
ultimately, you of you.

Suits

We think we're playing
with a full deck,
but we leave our hearts
at the door,
as we work with clubs
to bring home diamonds.
It all looks so black and white,
when the cards
have already been dealt,
but we have red
on our hands
from playing war too often
instead of bridge,
where we all win
in spades.

If Her House Could Talk

I see her,
pacing from room to room,
muttering thoughts
under her breath,
trying to figure everything out
when she knows what to do,
but doesn't
because she's too focused
on what she'll give up
rather than what she'll gain.
Only when
who she wants to be
outweighs clinging
onto old and accustomed ways
will new habits take root
and endure.

Takes One to Know One

He chose success over me,
others picked their
so-called freedom,
and you,
dare I say,
pledged your devotion
to the Heavens,
but these things
aren't mutually exclusive,
all of it rolling up into One,
as I now see
above the words,
gray clouds
blocking the daisies and rainbows,
and I can feel
how we all chose our fears
over love.

Juxtaposed

I'm right back
where I started.
Nothing has changed.
You made me believe
in something better
by balancing out the noise,
but it's still there,
and now,
I want to drown you out
for doing the cruelest thing of all,
making me believe
in something better.

Costly Trinkets

You have to forgive her
for her skepticism.
You see, she never had anyone
love the whole of her.
More like picking apart,
the parts of her
that they were initially attracted to,
now trying to be changed
or controlled,
until she leaves,
leaving them the souvenirs
that she doesn't find worthy
of bringing back home.

Bolder

Oh no,
not that!
I'd rather chew glass
or poke a fork
in my eyeball
than that!
I mean really,
just take a Sharpie and write
SUCKER
on my forehead.
I thought being bolder
meant being
unapologetically outspoken.
But nooooo.
It's much riskier than that,
mostly leading
to headaches and heartache.
Being bolder means being…
vulnerable.
Yep.
That's the worst.

Accepting the Unacceptable

I wake up
from the dream
where I'm hunkered down
in an underground storm shelter,
dark and dank,
feeling my way around
to find my way out,
only to turn around again
and see a light from above.

I move toward the brightness,
excited and eager,
barreling the cellar's door
wide open
only to feel the burn
from that,
that was supposed to heal.

Is accepting the unacceptable
acceptance
if nothing's impossible
in a world of infinite possibilities?

Keep Sake

You've created
a magical wonderland
and yet, at times
I see you struggling
to hang tight,
your world shaken…
again.

While others are transfixed
on your idyllic, picturesque world,
you keep hitting the wall,
trying to break free,
unable to extract yourself
from prying eyes.

Life in a snow globe
can encase you,
churn you up,
and make you feel small
and all you've ever wanted
is freedom.

The only way out
is within.

Tumbleweed

Boys set the rules,
girls follow them
to stay safe.
Safe...
like a prisoner
who gets a roof over her head
and three square meals a day.
Words blown around
these parts
like tumbleweed,
grasping on to those that hurt,
while the ones that don't
fall by the wayside.
It can all feel so hopeless sometimes,
yet the chains of life
will eventually give us
the freedom to fly.

Me

Beautiful intentions
fall flat
when they don't manifest
into actions.
All that I give,
not even noticed,
much less understood
by others.
I wish there was a me
for me.
Maybe the me
I'm seeking
is me.

The Wanter

The Wanter wants
what it wants,
what it asked for,
what it worked so hard for
and still didn't get.

I feel like I'm pushing
one of those shopping carts
that keeps veering left
when I want it to go right.
Do I really believe
I've come this far
to screw it up now?

Maybe the Wanter
doesn't know all.
Maybe veering left is right.
Maybe I need to not hold
onto the handle so tightly
and just allow it to lead me
to where I'm going.
Maybe I don't really know
what's in store.

PART 2: BURST

Untitled

I'm not who I used to be.
I'm who I always was.

The Heart Raptured

If I was Loveable...

what would I wear?
what would I eat?
what music would I listen to?
where would I go?
who would I hang out with?
how would I show up?
what would get my attention?
what would I act on?
what would I ignore?

And would it look like today?

A Stranger's Christmas Confession

He shared with me
how alone he was last Christmas, and
at the height of his loneliness,
he made a wish,
like a silent prayer,
that he didn't want
to celebrate another Christmas
like that again.
A year later,
he has his family
coming to visit,
a committed partner
who's carrying his child,
a son,
being born any day now,
due on Christmas Day,
the meaningfulness of all this
not lost on him.
I got everything I asked for...and more.
His animation suddenly
turned to shyness
and he ended our chance encounter muttering,
I don't even know why I'm telling you all this,
but...I do.

Write Combination

There is a lock
on the splintered door
of the withered heart.
It's seen its share of battles.
Though I try
to open the lock
with the write combination
only you can walk
through the cobwebs,
down heart's staircase
and open the chambers
to feel again.

Chalking It Up

I see myself
in my elementary school classroom,
erasing the big, green chalkboard
in the front of the class.
Never the teacher's pet,
she picked me
from the group
to do the hardest job,
erasing my pain
line by line
until all that's left
is a clean slate
and a blank state.

Feeling Your Way Home

Rejection without acceptance
is called suffering.
Rejection with acceptance
is called freedom.
Rejecting yourself
is called hiding.
Rejecting others
is called self-preservation.
Rejecting rejection is called forgiveness.
A world without rejection
is called love.

August

Sleepy summer days
are coming to a close,
time to harvest
the fruits of surrender.

Wake up!
We've got work to do.
The ever growing seeds of trust
now need to bloom.

It's time to save the world,
one heart at a time,
starting with you.

Me and You

I love who I am
when I'm with You.

I hate who I am
when I'm with *you*.

But what's most important
is Me loving me,
regardless of *you* and You.

Summers in the Catskills

When most folks we knew
headed south to the shore,
my family packed up
our brown Buick station wagon
and drove north to the mountains.

My recollections of those times,
when days went on for miles,
are like sketchy snapshots
fastened to a swirling pinwheel.
My grandpa mowing the waist-high grass.
Picking blueberries that we collected
in empty paper milk cartons
with the tops cut off and string attached
so they hung around our necks like lanterns.
Curling up on a dusty couch
reading old books off the shelves.
Finding buttercups and holding them
under our chins to reveal truths
and picking petals off of daisies
with he loves me, he loves me not.

And though my memories are scattered
like autumn leaves on the ground,
to my senses they are indelible and ever-present,
bringing me back to those carefree days.
Like the sound of crickets
that lull me to sleep on a hot, humid night.
The musty smell of book stores and old furniture.
The taste of my Dad's blueberry jam
he continues to make every year.
And the hugs from my family
that still make me feel
safe, supported, and loved
wherever and whenever we are.

Grief Revisited

I know it's not easy,
but resisting the memories
of those you've loved and lost
is like having them die twice.
By sitting with the stories
and listening to your songs,
you can choose
to bathe in the tender feelings
that wash over you,
so by loving others
as you had them,
you keep their love alive.

Wishful Thinking

I wish I had
one more day
with you.
Nothing too crazy
or serious.
Just lots of playfulness,
laughter, and hugs,
without the knowledge
that this would be
our last moments together,
because it would be
way too hard
to say goodbye to you.

Oh wait…
in hindsight,
I did get my wish,
after all.

Hands Together Now

Her words
hang in silence,
buoyed and unencumbered
on plain white paper
because even lines
feel invasive
for the unsung melodies
of her cursive verses.
It's more than a feeling.
It is.
Her hands outstretched,
then cupped together,
and finally
palms pressed together.

The gift is within your hands.

Angled for Possibilities

Belief is stronger than thought,
but weaker than the whispers
of the soul.
Beliefs give way to meaning,
the mind making
numerous interpretations
to a single event,
while the heart knows
the only reason is love.

Just Say Know

You're not asking me to believe.
Rather to trust
my inner knowings,
since beliefs,
even good ones,
are constructed
from the confinements
of the mind,
while knowings
are truths
that bubble up
from the heart,
earthing spirit.

Her

She apologized to me
for hiding out
for so long,
leaving me
to fend for myself
in the world.
And now that she's back,
we're inseparable,
melding into each other
to form something new
and beautiful,
becoming One.

My Child,

Don't make it
your mission in life
to seek my approval
because you could never
displease me.

In fact, when who you really are
shows up in our day to day,
it tastes like a sweet burst of chocolate
with the surprise filling in the middle,
as we only taste the sour
when we try to be who we're not.

So continue to amaze me
around every corner we take
instead of conforming to my vision of you.
I know, at times,
I don't show you this sentiment,
when I'm lost
in my own not enoughness,
and you,
just by your mere presence,
are always more than that.

Teach me who you are
and I promise
to do so for you
as well.

Dream Weaver

In this time and space
there is a place
where all lifelines go.
Some string along,
while others are strung out,
but for us,
as we move closer together
are becoming intertwined,
woven into something new,
altogether.

The Naked I

Now that you've shown us
who we truly are,
whole, complete, and enough,
play for us
the melody, rhythm, and rhyme
of how we truly are,
acceptance, belonging, and connectedness,
created from the purist simplicity
of why we are,
the full and bare
disclosure of love.

Growing a Bamboo Heart

Puddling,
evidence of the heart melting.

A heart of ice is strong,
but brittle
as it cracks
under the weight
of pain,
the smooth, cold surface
keeps the hurt
and everything else out,
so as not to agitate or add
to the current ache
it keeps within
its solid fragility.

But a late spring
is the cause
for the current thaw,
where water's frigid strength
shatters
and becomes bendable
like bamboo,
the greatest resistance
to resistance,
and in its place,
a heart replaced,
from dying in the frozen weeds
to living among the never-ending
ever-growing reeds,
a discerning inclusivity
where everything is seen,

clear, crisp, centered, and focused
with soft and fuzzy edges
blurring into every,
swathed and swaddled
in softness.

Take heart and flourish
at nothing,
at all.

Letting the World In

I'd close the front door
to keep others out.
I'd slam the front door
to deal with conflict.
I'd examine the front door
to figure out what was wrong with it.
I'd take the front door off its hinges
to replace it with something better.

Today,
I gently opened the front door
and let the breeze, sounds, and scents
pour through the screen door
like a sieve
and assault my senses,
letting myself feel all of it.

Funny, a moth got in somehow.
Must have been attracted to my light,
now flamed
by the kerosene of intimacy.

Gift Returns

Gifts come in all shapes and sizes,
but my gift to you
is expansive and ethereal,
the gift that keeps giving
without ever being fully received
though it's always enough.

Not the Fountain of Youth,
though it makes you feel
young and eternal,
a gift you can offer
to yourself and others,
coming and going,
everflowing.

A gift so mysterious and present
it's right in front of you,
in you,
and through you,
though beautifully hidden
and deeply felt.

The gift of you,
through my eyes
when all I see is love.

A Perspective Textured

Sketches

I'm not saying
to deny what happened.
All I'm asking
is for a shift in perspective,
from fear to love,
to color your meaning
of the events
from black and white
to shades of gray.

The Scribe and the Sage

I'm really just a
rabbit eared antenna,
placed high and crooked,
on top of an old black and white
Zenith TV,
receiving signals from above
and writing them down.
These transmissions
usually arrive
at the most inopportune times,
which explains
why I have love notes
throughout my house, car and purse,
written on notebook paper, napkins
and the backs of receipts,
sometimes in crayon or lipstick
when need be,
until I have time to transfer it
to a more respectable mode of documentation.
So you see,
I'm just the scribe,
and you,
the sage.

The Tease

I reach out to you,
to nourish
this anemic heart.
Hands cupped around you,
drinking in your essence,
feeling the warmth
of our unhurried embrace.
A cup of tea
on a hot summer night
to get the chill
out of the artificial air.
Life isn't always
what it seems.

This is How it Works

We think we're so clever,
figuring everything out
getting to choose what's best.

We don't get to choose
because fate
has already been mapped out
regardless of how well we plan.

We don't need to choose
because there is no one right way,
regardless of how we agonize
over the impact
of our decisions.

All we need to do
is get quiet
and listen
and choose
in each moment
how we react
and respond
to the unchosen.

Victor

They're singing your praises,
but you can't hear them
because it's hard to receive
what you don't believe.

Don't let the mocking birds
keep you grounded.
They're all just vultures
trying to find their next prey,
anyway.
Just keep spreading your wings,
flocking with birds of the same feather.

Remember, birds with clipped wings
can still take flight.

Minimizing Misperceptions

With an open heart
and a blank mind,
find out the why
behind the what
before you assume,
because what you're thinking
probably isn't true anyway.

Intention is relevant.

Floored

Knotted, stained, and sealed,
from glossy to flat,
until sanded down
to the subfloor,
the deconstruction of me
takes me from hard would
to being totally floored,
out to the beveled edge,
all decked out for One.

Game Changer

Receiving without misperceiving,
seeing without disbelieving,
knowing without rereading,
meaning without bleeding.
The only way to win
is how you play the game.

The Fighter

You come out swinging,
but I don't fight back
because you are me
and I am you.
So how can I hit back?
Sometimes, the best shot
is the one not taken.

Besides, I know
when the crowds are gone
and the gloves come off
that you don't really hate me.
You hate you.

And though I feel your blows,
they hurt you more
than they hurt me.
When you can see that
then you'll give up the fight
with me,
and most importantly,
with you.

Tug-of-War

Almost as old as time,
the push and pull
of the other
on the other,
each going nowhere,
until a muddy victor emerges,
worn and bruised
from the battle.

But if one side
decides
to stop the struggle
by letting go
of the frayed rope
too soon,
the other topples
while still claiming victory.

Yet, if both sides
put down the cord
that we're all entwined in,
at the same time,
well then,
the games are finally over.

What Then?

What if I'm not
who I was?
What if the past
doesn't define who I am?
What if I don't believe
what others think of me,
and stand in my Truth,
not in the shadows of mediocrity
revealing my anonymity.
What then?

The Masquerade

Veiled words
and cloaked actions
are eventually revealed
from its phantom disguise
because the truth
is always visible
to those who are intimate
with the unmasked.

Projector

The movies
in our minds
are no match
for the images
being projected
onto one another.
I'm less of what
you think of me
and more than
you'll ever know.

Repurposed

Everything
that used to
bring me joy
is still beautiful,
but when your happiness
is sourced from within,
it all looks
a little lackluster
while keeping
its original shine.

Liberation

Perception is reality
but not necessarily the Truth.
I don't want to change
my decision.
I want to change
your reaction.
Like a snake
shedding its skin
leaving the hollowed out carcass behind,
it slithers away,
exposed,
but not
unprotected.

Connecting

The ones who resist
are the ones
who feel
they don't deserve.

When I disconnect from you,
I disconnect from God.
When I disconnect from you,
I disconnect from me.

New eyes
see broken pieces
of shattered glass.
Your love defied time
by touching me here.

Making a Spectacle of Herself

Since taking off
her rose-colored glasses,
her days have been unusually stark,
but on the bridge
of her knows
sits a new pair of shades
that eclipses the shadows,
her world
now karmically colored,
as she roams into the vulnerable open,
seeing clearly
while drinking in the sun.

Double Vision

I grabbed my telescope
to see more clearly,
but when I looked
through the lens,
the view was distorted
with new patterns,
symmetrical and precise,
a beautiful dance of mirrored angles
that changed shapes
with a slight shift
of hand and perspective,
like time itself.
Unbeknownst to me,
a kaleidoscope
provided a better view
of how things really are.

Virtual Bifocals

I have a form,
but I'm not my body.
I have thoughts,
but I'm not my mind.
I have feelings,
but I'm not my emotions.
I live in the world
with no edges,
near and far sighted.

The Man In the Moon

By sleight of hand
and shift of gaze,
try angles merge
into a circled sphere,
where phases of life
are revealed,
finally out of hiding,
basking in the glow
earthed by the sun.
And who, pray tell,
isn't moonstruck
by the sight
of an entity
in all its fullness.

I to I

When we choose to see
from the eyes of abundance,
there is more for all.

When we choose to see
from the eyes of scarcity,
there is less for me.

Causing a Seen

With tunnel vision,
you can't fully see
the scenes
beyond the edges
into the edgeless,
where there is no acceptance
without forgiveness,
no knowing
without unknowing,
no one right way
when there's only One.

Maybe

Sometimes the welcomed answer
to the reverent question
isn't yes or no.
Sometimes it's maybe.
Sometimes maybe is ambitious,
not just avoidance.
Sometimes maybe is coy,
not just noncommittal.
Sometimes maybe is strong,
not just wishy washy.
Sometimes maybe is hopeful,
not just discouraging.
Sometimes maybe is better
than an untrue yes
or a defiant no.
Sometimes, it does depend.
Maybe,
just maybe.

Butterfly Effect

I know things
I really shouldn't know.
I feel things
I don't understand.
I see near and far,
but am missing
the middle piece
of how I get there.

Is this the beginning
of the end
or the beginning
of my becoming?

Hues

We're different.
More like a watercolor
than oil and water.

Colors,
bleeding into each other,
soaking in each other's differences
in shades, techniques, and tones
with no hard edges,
flat wash, or staining.
Simply smooth strokes on rough paper,
textured, versatile, flexible,
with depth and dimension
all contributing to craft a masterpiece.

I wish life could imitate art.

Breaking Myths

You can't have it all,
but you can have
what you want.

Do you know what this?

My sense is that you do.
You simply don't believe you can
have it,
do it,
be it.
And you can.

Wishes

Be careful
what you wish for
because you will get it,
just not necessarily
how you envisioned.
So different
from what you thought
that sometimes
you don't even realize
you have your wish…
until you do.

Be careful
what you wish for
because there is no time frame
for making them come true.
If there was,
you'd have it by now,
and then you'd begin wishing
for something else.

Friday Night

I know.
I'm sitting here
by myself,
but I'm not alone.
I'd feel more lonely
in the middle of the crowd,
at least for tonight anyway.
I like the company I keep.
Isn't that what we ultimately want?
And besides,
I'm not alone.

Both

I used to think
life was like
a thunderstorm
on a hot, summer afternoon,
finding relief
from the oppressive air
and stifling heat.

All the while,
wanting to feel life
like a freshly laundered sheet,
hanging on the line,
flapping in the breeze.

And tonight,
watching a thunderstorm
from my bedroom,
lying on freshly laundered sheets,
I'm sensing it's both.

Cross Country

Are you proud of me?
she whispered.
I thought this was put to rest
a few hours ago,
but she still had her doubts.
She couldn't understand
how I could be applauding her
when she came in second to last
because she doesn't yet recognize
that the How
is as important
as the What,
and for those who don't remember,
well, winning can come at a big price.

So sweet child,
with hard work and perseverance,
you finished what you started
while remaining a team player,
even when things looked bleak.
Are you proud of me?
A child's never-ending question,
at any age,
and though you didn't win
that race this time,
you won the greatest race of all,
the human one.

ADHD

When a minority
is at the tipping point
of becoming mainstream,
we need to rethink
how we define this *disorder*
and reclaim it
as evolution.

There's nothing wrong with you.
Just a mismatch
with this augmented reality
where disruptive innovation
isn't conventional.

What if
instead of being labeled
developmentally delayed
you were actually
ahead of your time?

Peripheral Vision

They view me
as being lazy and unambitious
when I'm playing small,
but I know
I'm observing, taking notes,
learning.

They accuse me
of being pretentious and conceited
when I'm playing big,
but I know I'm practicing,
perfecting my craft,
taking the slow and bumpy ride
to mastery,
nothing big or small about it,
my manner filled
with touches of joyful self-satisfaction,
not rubs of smug dissatisfaction.

But then again,
their perceptions
of all
are divided,
so they only see
the parts of me
that they see in themselves,
while I envision
the whole of us.

Her Pandora's Box

She keeps digging…
for years,
searching for the
buried time capsule
that's impacting her todays.
Digging,
until her shovel
meets Earth's core,
and hits something foreign
and familiar.
As she lifts the container
from the dirt,
she doesn't know
what will pain her more,
the remnants found
in her chest
or the realization
that the box
has been empty
all along.

Colander

Thin-skinned and filtered,
people, places, and things
sieved through the poked holes
of our existence
until all that remains
is the unrestrained strainer.
It was never about
our time here,
but what we leave behind.

For our Daughters...and Sons

Life can feel like
a tug of war,
a tight rope,
opposing sides pulling
with all their might,
back and forth,
until one side gains ground
when the other loses their footing
pulling harder yet,
until the other is weaker and weaker.

Life is but a reflection
of our relationship
with ourselves,
the ego and soul.

The world is a reflection
of the collective consciousness
of each individual relationship.

Coming to neutral terms
with our current reality
clears the negativity
that clouds thoughts and judgments
and leads to different actions
that support change,
for ALL.

Accepting what is
doesn't mean passivity
and silencing the unwilling partner
isn't the way
to our heart's desires.
If you want to do something
to move the needle
in the direction of what you seek,
you've got to be at the table,
invited or not.

Vacancy

Invisible,
they act like they don't see me.
Maybe they can't
or choose not to.
Regardless, I see what could be in others,
but if they don't want to be that,
then this dreamer
momentarily turned realist,
doesn't have to pretend
it's anything more than this.
Feeling like a houseguest
who's overstayed her welcome,
it's time to strip the bed,
pack up my stuff
and say my goodbyes.
Faith is listening
to the whispers of my inner voice
gently nudging me on
instead of
the blaring sirens of reason
telling me otherwise.

The Ruby Slippers

When things don't go as planned
and you find yourself
in the eye of a tornado,
there's no need to run away
or wish for what's over the rainbow
for things to be different.
During your travels
down the yellow brick road of life,
be aware of advice
from wizards
when you can't see
what's behind the curtain,
and don't be surprised
to receive kindness
from witches.
Use your brain
to orient yourself,
when at an unfamiliar crossroad,
to find your next direction
away from the fire.
Keep your heart well-oiled
so it doesn't rust,
even during an unexpected storm.
Find your courage
when facing your fears of
lions, tigers and bears.
And never, ever
underestimate the power
of a cool pair of shoes
and how you saunter in them
to find your way back Home.

PART 3: FLEURISH

Picking Flow'ers

It's okay to pick and choose
who you share
your Truth with.
Not everyone can handle
the flourish.

A New Journey Ventured

Stretching Exercise

You can step
out of your comfort zone
when you realize
there is none.

Silhouettes

I never realized
how little space I consumed
keeping myself in line,
living straight and narrow,
in the corner
of a perfect 90 degrees,
that didn't measure up
to who I really am,
a circle
in a rectangular world
that triangles outside
its contours
for a different life
to take shape.

Coin Toss

Adrift and bereft,
unsure of where I'm heading,
but...what I do know
is that
this way isn't it.

After grasping and clinging
I decided to leave
it all behind,
but they're both really
just flip sides
of the same attachment coin
since walking away
doesn't necessarily mean
letting go.

But a shift
to the middle
can create different outcomes,
like how forgiveness
leads to acceptance,
patience
to kindness,
gratitude
to abundance,
and humility
to truly and finally
letting go.

The Soloist

For too long,
I've tried out for the team,
auditioned for the part,
attempted to blend in with the chorus,
without much success.
It's time to take center stage,
step into the spotlight
and own the role
that was written for me
and play to an audience
of One.

Leaving a Legacy

Not accepted in their world.
Don't belong in mine.
Doors shut
on what I thought I wanted.
Windows opened
on what I thought I didn't.
Shoved here,
jostled there,
gliding through wide bends,
pausing at sharp turns,
unexpectedly rerouted,
a zig zag journey
down a rocky trail
toward destiny,
with the choices of free will
determining the path
to no final destination.

Caveat Emptor

You sold me a lie
and I believed you
because you were wiser and older,
and who doesn't want to be happy.

But it didn't work that way for me
and for years
I thought there was something wrong
with ME,
and maybe
it didn't work for you either
and you just didn't have the awareness,
forethought, or courage
to live any differently.

But now that I'm branching out,
you gingerly place your fears in my lap
to dissuade me from dissenting
from the safety of conformity.
And yet you!
You were the one
who told me I could be
whatever I wanted to become,
but I guess that's only if
it conforms with your vision of me.

No more.
There's nothing safe
about any of this,
only of that.

The 100th Monkey

How crafty is the practice
of spreading unquestioned falsehoods
under the name of righteousness,
when there's nothing right about it,
supplying a slow and steady stream
or slap of hand
erosion of credibility
on its target
who speaks her truth
that is different than their own.

Common practice to these affronts
is to dim the frequency of one's light
to dissuade the punishment
of rejection and social alienation
by those who want to keep
our high vibrations low.

But social change will come
when enough of us
stop drinking the spirits
that we're taught to drink
for our merriment,
that only lessens our own.

An insider,
living inside out,
I don't know
if I'll make it out of here
in one piece this time,
but I'll always remain whole,
untouchable,
shining bright
all the way down
to our demise.

Veteran

I know you didn't expect
to be a causality
in the latest battle
of the mind,
but the war is over
and I'm marching through
and out of the scorched remains,
not looking back.

A-Void-Dance

Pick your head up
and out
from the quicksand
you put it in…
and deal.

There can be fairness
and inclusivity
in the untamed wildness,
now cloaked in righteousness
and civility,
but not by your choice
of avoidance.
There's no denying destiny.

Realm of Possibility

Laughter fills my consciousness,
springing from the realm of possibility
where potential melds with destiny.
Fighting destiny
is called free will.
Flowing with destiny
is called fate.
Destiny isn't a choice.
It just is.
What we choose
is how we get there.

LED Lights

Plugged in,
powered up
to light the world,
and yet again,
you remain hard wired,
accusing me of faulty lines
for the cause
of the latest energy crisis,
when really,
you crossed a live wire
with your broken connection,
leaving me in a blackout.

The light bulb finally went off
in my head,
so instead of blowing a fuse,
changing circuits,
or going off the grid,
I'm alternating currents now,
changing the negative ions
that's been going on for eons
into the positive,
because I can see the futility
in the utility company
I'm keeping.

So the spark plug
that insulated me
from your resistance
to my magnetic field
has been recalibrated,
amped up,
bolted by high voltage
by my own power supply,
sourced from within,
shining on.

Jewel Thief

You stole years from me
by keeping me tucked away
in your safe
to keep you safe,
while taking me out on special occasions
so I could cast my light on you,
enlivening you,
a prized accessory.

But now that I know my worth,
I'm out of hiding,
shining bright
all glittered and bejeweled.
And though you accuse me
of being tarnished and gaudy,
you can't diminish
what is mine.

I own my light,
it's not on consignment anymore,
and maybe the jewel thief
was me all along.

Raptured

I can appreciate
how receiving
their highs and lows
enflamed by lack
is more tantalizing
than my steady stream
of enoughness.
So please understand
when my acceptance
of what is
renders not tolerating…
anymore.

Acceptance
doesn't necessarily mean
staying.

Ex-Contortionist

I'm doing it again.
Thinking of ways
to win you over
and change your mind
about me.
I almost did it too,
but I sense the futility
in that.
I'm learning,
slowly,
how to walk away.

Haunted

Your voice echoed
through the room.
You swore to me
that your face
would be the last
I'd ever see here.
I remained silent,
replying back only
with a firm stance
and soft eyes
before I walked away
from you forever.
And now, you've become
a forgotten travel log,
collecting dust in an old scrapbook
of what was,
while you keep replaying that scene
over and over,
your prophesy self-fulfilling,
a curse of sorts,
whose spell only you can break.
I think my silence
is what haunts you the most.

Marionette

They first teach you
to want these things
to be successful,
then show you
how you need these things
to be happy,
and then they
string you along
by pulling your purse strings
to perform the hollow victory dance.
Cut the strings
and do what makes
your soul dance
and plunge towards
your biggest downfall
and greatest windfall.

Internal Compass

I can feel the chill
breeze through
the partially closed window,
now facing South.
The winds of change
are in the air,
moving East to West,
where the window of opportunity
is opening,
in the direction of True North.

Calling In What's Next

Give me the awareness
to let the past go,
the clarity to know when
I'm resisting what is,
the strength to release habits
that don't serve me anymore,
and the faith to live
in the not knowing.

Lighthouse

Alone,
standing tall,
shining bright,
night after night,
helping travelers
find their way home.
Is it enough for you
or do you secretly wish
for more?

Treasure Hunt

My head says 80/20.
My heart says 50/50.

My head says Fall.
My heart says Summer.

My head says either/or.
My heart says and.

My head is confused.
My heart totally gets it.

Life's map,
sprinkled with clues,
makes this reality treasure hunt
all the more magical,
don't you think…

Lost and Found

You lost
a most precious belonging
on your walk home
last evening.
Oh, how sad you were,
and how ironic
that the actions you took
to prevent this situation
was actually it's cause.
But you did nothing wrong,
except for maybe possessing
a healthy dose
of youthful innocence.
So this may be
the experience
to help you remember
to be trusting
and aware,
especially about the few things
in this world
that are most precious to you.
So come, my precious
and let's go find it
together.

Oasis

A nomad
traveling through the desert,
until you stumble upon a home
that nourishes you
and brings you comfort, joy, and beauty
that you then decorate others with
through your work
that feels like a tall glass of cold water
to all the other wanderers
still roaming through the desert.
You're not homeless.
It's not hopeless.
It just is.
And it's okay.

The Challenger

It's better
that I don't know
the rules of the game
or aspire to follow them
blindly.
Being limited to what's possible
makes everything impossible
and that's a game
I never want to play.

Sun Glare

Best you not forget
that not everyone
has your best interests
at heart.
Not because they're bad
or that you're not enough.
It's just that
some feel the burn,
not the warmth
of your brightness.
But you needn't stop shining.
Simply find respite
in the cool shade
you're co-creating.

Coming True

Did you ever have a dream
of what could be?
A dream so real
you can see it,
smell it,
touch it?
A dream so big
you can't even fathom
how it's going to come true?
A dream so crazy and out there,
you recognize that
you have to do things differently
and yet, you don't even know
where to start?
A dream so inconceivable
that you have to let go
of the constructs in your mind
telling you it's impossible?
Then, and only then,
through surrendered actions
will it come true.

Yes...especially then.

The Manifestor

Sure,
there's a magical mystical component
to all this,
but I can't explain it to you.
It's just something I feel,
like playing the kid's game
Hot and Cold,
I get colder the farther away
and warmer the closer I get
to the desired.
All I know in making the impossible,
possible,
is to chunk down my dreams, hopes, and wishes
from an overwhelming, unrealistic place
into something believable,
in the form of small, actionable steps.
If you do that multiple times
every day,
day after day,
something's bound to happen.

Displaced

An emotional hostage
finally unchained,
only to become
a fugitive on the run,
now a refugee,
seeking asylum,
finding her way
to freedom.

Tag, You're It!

In the playground of the mind,
my seven year old self is giggling,
enjoying the chase,
the thrill of not getting caught,
running with glee
around the lone tree
in the field where we'd all meet up.

The magical willow tree,
lush and curvy,
with a thick trunk
that served its purpose of home base
in addition to other childhood wonders
like climbing its limbs,
and getting lost in the maze
of its droopy branches and elongated leaves.

Years later,
I still feel the chase,
but it isn't so much fun anymore,
the safety and security
of home base elusive.
Until the day I stopped and stood there
and became the tree
becoming my own home base,
the game finally over.

The Ruse

Sharp as a tack
that bursts the bubble
I was trying
to get out of anyway,
and yet every time
I stretched almost beyond,
it snapped me back
into the fetal position,
waiting for me
to be reborn.

Punctured and perforated,
not as a punishment,
but as a wake up call,
these tests of will
are all a ruse
to self-discovery,
to return to the self.

They may decide
if the ruse worked,
but only you determine
if you passed.

The Entrepreneurial Instinct

Most days
there are moments
of self-doubt, uncertainty,
and disbelief,
but you plunge in anyway.
The feelings evoked
from the meaning,
purpose, and vision
of what you're embarking on
outweighs the fear.
And besides, you know
you're too far down
the rabbit hole
to turn back now.

Capturing Hearts

You pay them
to show up and produce.
You spark their imagination
with ideas
so they can contribute,
but capturing hearts
with the belief in them
and of something better
will lead others to march
to the beat of inspiration,
even in the face of
uncertainty and adversity
of realizing.

New Year's Blessing

Visualize yourself
standing like a tall tree,
with your feet rooted into the ground,
and your arms raised to the sky.
Heaven on Earth converge.

As you look down the road,
are you contemplating the path taken,
or imagining the journey ahead?

At the twilight of the year,
we are inclined to take stock
of the seeds we planted
and what came to fruition…
and what did not.

As we look ahead,
with hope and anticipation
at what may come into bloom
in the coming days and beyond,
I wish you a present
filled with blessings of love and peace
at what is.

The Start of Something Good

I'm on the brink
of realizing
all that I've worked so hard for,
when,
out of nowhere,
I feel the urge to…
pause.
Funny how I'm stopping now,
an inch away from achieving
a major milestone
towards this never-ending finish line,
but I'm suddenly feeling nostalgic
for what is,
knowing it will soon be
what was,
and not knowing
what will be.
Everything is temporary and timeless.
Even this.

A Good Cry

You did it.
After all the
learning and doing,
asking and deciding,
practicing and failing,
success has finally come your way.
And with victory comes
invitations, celebrations, and attention.
But in the sliver of time
between right now
and what's next,
don't be surprised
to find yourself
alone,
having a good cry,
for all that you were,
all that you are,
and all that you're becoming.

Rue

Skimming stones
instead of skipping stones,
the time spent wishing
I was somewhere else,
when I was where
I was supposed to be,
to get to where I'm at,
so I can grow
into who I want to be.

The Reluctant Activist

I know situations
threw you into a role
you weren't planning to fill.
And though the days
can feel long and tired,
igniting social change
is never a waste of time
just because it hasn't been
realized yet.
You're not alone
as you forge out into the world,
creating a sense of belonging
by connecting with similar peeps
who share your vision
of what can be.
You're demonstrating
a show of strength and solidarity
to the opposition
that you're a force to be reckoned with.
And you begin changing
the silent majority
that are sitting on the fence,
watching every ripple
you make.

Tiger Lilies

You can imagine my shock
when I got home
and they were gone,
excavated and annihilated,
for being naturally unruly,
accused of ruining
the well-manicured landscape.

So you can imagine my surprise
when a year and a day later
they grew back,
returned and rebirthed.
Don't they know
that the wild and wonderful
can never be extinguished.

High Heeled Through the Storm

As they run for shelter,
I keep walking
like I own the place,
uncovered,
the rain pelting down
on me.

Despite the rumors
that I'll melt
right then and there
on the sidewalk
by the mere touch of water,
I continue my stroll,
even though I'm probably ruining
my new silk blouse
at this very moment.

With my clothes
clinging to my body,
my hair plastered
to my head,
and whatever makeup I have
left on my face
after this crazy day
streaked across my cheeks,
I keep walking in long, slow strides,
transfixed on the rain
rather than the stream
of jagged stares.

I just couldn't stop.
I haven't felt this alive
in a long time.

You Can't Judge a Book By Its Cover

The smell of new,
ink and glue,
guided me
to the new releases,
and the display
didn't disappoint.
Creaseless covers,
book after book,
lined in rows
with straight spines,
binds unbroken,
I felt the usual swoosh
of excitement
come over me,
knowing my next adventure
into a new world
was about to take off.

But as I get closer,
I see one of the same
in the far right corner,
weary from its travels,
its corners frayed,
a stain on the bottom,
and a whole chapter bent.
In that moment, I knew
no one would by this book
so I picked it up
before it got discarded.

As I went to pay,
the cashier gently reminded me
that there were books
in better condition
than the one I chose.
No I said,
I want this one.
He then graciously offered me
a discount
for being damaged,
but I declined that too,
because I knew its worth,
it speaking to me
before it was even read.

Tattered and worn
on the outside,
but still the same juiciness
on the inside,
it survived its journey
and found its way home.

A Life Nonforfeitured

Freedom of Choice

You can't
take anything
from me
when I need nothing
from you.

Full Moon

I ran by the glow
of the moon
in the predawn.
It followed me
down each street,
the warmth of its presence
welcoming against the backdrop
of the cold, still air
in the lonely, dark hours.
I asked the moon for help,
knowing it could relate
to the cyclical nature
of my need to know,
and at the end of my run,
when the sun was just peeking
through the horizon,
it dawned on me
that the sweet moon
was the answer all along.

The Skeptic

I know you think
this is all so wooey woo
and dippity doo,
an easy mark
for target practice.
I get it because
I've been there before myself,
but belief, faith, and trust
doesn't have to make sense
for it to be real.
And I don't feel the need
to convince you of anything
because there is no either/or.
So come, sit,
and have a cup of tea with me
and we'll just be.

Witches

These days…
we don't have a noose
around our necks,
just hung out to dry.
We're not burned at the stake,
just fired from our jobs, and
we don't get stoned to death,
just words hurled our way
killing our reputation.

Regardless of what they think,
we can't just concoct a magic potion
to break the spell of
us versus them, and
right or wrong.
Though we aren't locked
in a dungeon anymore
we remain locked
in the prison of the mind.

So sweet girl,
come out and play.
It's not that
the dragons went away.
It's just now
you know how to slay them.
The one that was banished
for not blending in
is now freed
from the chambers of the heart.

Afraid and fearless,
she's got a lot to say
and she's not banished anymore.
The one who was dragged
out of her home
by an angry mob with torches
can be killed, but
will never die.
It's that knowing
that scares them so.
So?

Hunters and Gatherers

You question
what I do
to everyone but me,
accuse me of being
"too emotional" at work,
and no,
I'm not sleeping with the boss.
I got where I am
because I'm good,
and I know that now,
and based on your actions,
so do you.

You can try to diminish
my light,
but you can't extinguish
the distinguished
because I am
that good.

Faking Her Own Death

Heroine,
heralding in
the new knew,
caped and cloaked
because even superheroes
hide their identities
while defending good.
But in the end,
she couldn't change
the untruths
so she chose instead
to play into them
because she'd rather
be the hero of her own story
than typecast as the villain
in yours.

Members Only

When we lose ourselves
to gain acceptance from others,
we never truly feel
like we belong.
When personal freedoms
are comprised,
we're talking about a revolution.
So I'm starting
my own secret society
of One.
Wanna join?

Unleashed

A white collar,
attached to a gold chain,
tethered by a long leash,
the reward for executing
a near perfect performance
every time.

But she grew dog-tired
of her glittered cage.

Drained from constantly
learning a new trick,
chasing her tail,
or playing dead,
she knew she had to lick this life
even before she sniffed out
exactly what's next,
prepared to fight
for every scrap.

A show dog,
labeled a stray,
gone astray,
and all she knows for sure is,
though it isn't easy,
doggone it,
she's finally free.

Making Cent$

I'm not bankrupt or netted,
more going for broke,
so please don't be naïve
to think I don't know
or that I'm in denial
that I didn't earn what I have.
The price of freedom
does come steep -
at the cost of one's reputation,
or so I thought
until recently,
when you were credited
and I was discounted,
again,
that I finally balanced the account
knowing that Truth
always gets its asking price
and you can't afford me.

Finding Her Voice

She calls it
like she sees it,
and unknowingly
triggers you
into making her
the scapegoat
for your pain,
shooting the messenger,
while,
she keeps shooting
for the stars,
unsure, but unharmed
by your weapon of words,
she continues making shots,
instead of taking them.

Taking Her Lead

She didn't ask to be
the latest target
of the uproar,
the one she caused
by calling them out
on their bad behavior.
By moving out
and moving on,
she may have lost some pride,
but found in its place
a renewed faith in herself.

They think the problem
is now gone,
but some folks never learn
or find out the hard way,
that she is the ultimate vanquisher.

Right?

Write what you want to say
and not what you think
they want to hear.

Right what you want to do
and not what you think
they want to see.

Rite what you love
and not what you think
they want you to believe.

Inkblot

The ink is running dry.
The quill has stopped
its fervent dance
over the papered surface,
running out
of things to write
because I've found my voice
in everything I do.

Chocolate Bloom

She invited me in,
a sweet tooth
of a friend,
her house decorated in chocolate,
matching her current vibe
after the years of hard candy
she's chewed on,
she didn't torte herself
a hazelnut
sitting around
eating bonbons all day.
Instead, she pralined
her caked on, baked in,
semisweet coating
into something untried,
untruffled,
soft, and gooey,
her outside now finally blended
with her inside filling.

Border Lines

First they teach you
to draw inside the lines,
then they correct you
until you learn your lines,
but after toeing the line
it's time
to go offline
because life lines
are really about
rising up
and righting down
on the unlined surface
that's surfaced.
That's where
you'll leave your mark.

Well-To-Do

I saw him pray
to the Money God
with a get-rich-quick scheme
so he could buy cool stuff
to impress others,
and himself.

But I believe
in the Abundance God
where there is plenty
in all
with all.

And though he's making a killing,
I've got the golden touch
because even with
my broader scope
and longer timespan
to break the bank,
he's still seeking, searching
and I'm already set for life.

On the Dock

I know you're tired,
treading water
for a long time now.
I keep trying
to save you,
but you keep
pulling me down
underwater
to barely stay afloat.
I'm not doing that anymore.
I'll be your lifeguard,
and you,
your life preserver.

Untangling Nots

I'm not going to keep saying
I'm sorry to you anymore
when I'm being faithful to me.

I'm not going to reject myself
before you reject me anymore
because the thoughts
that prevent me
from reaching out to you
are what's holding me back.

I'm not going to try
and change your negative perceptions
of me anymore
because my reputation in life
becomes my legacy in death,
all mostly untrue anyway.

I'm not going to let
your not lovely ways
trigger me anymore
because it's how you play,
rather than what you win,
that ultimately defines success.

I'm not going to harden myself
to be unfeeling towards you anymore
because I can take off my armor
and not be caught off guard,
vulnerable,
not defenseless.

I'm not going to make myself small
so you're more comfortable
with me anymore
because regardless of whatever I do
you keep wanting less and less of me
and I can disappear on my own terms.

I'm not going to give in
to my vices
to deal with you anymore,
because I can recover easier now,
not having to artificially cope with life
when I'm living more authentically.

I forgave you
because I forgive me.

A Reconstructed Breast Stroke

She dives right in
to most things
on solid ground,
but not in the
unsteady stream of water
after feeling the sting
of the belly flop
in the lake
long ago.

She doesn't feel the need
to learn now
since she sees
where going head first
can lead to,
but she does admit
she never was able
to control the flood
of feelings
overflowing since then,
except to dam the gush
inside her heart
so tight,
that it eventually bubbled up
and out
of her chest
into a form of a lump
that had to be cut away.

Afterwards,
the ones who should know
said she was cured,
but she knew
deep down
she was still treading water,
not able to support herself
in the tides of emotions,
until one unremarkable day,
she felt the urge to randomly
put her big toe
in the pool,
and started to build her strength,
slowly,
until she gradually
graduated to the backstroke
to examine and reframe
what was coiled so tight
around her scarred torso.

And now, she's won
her own race,
not theirs,
gracefully and graciously
swimming freestyle.

Soldier On

She gets ready,
her lipstick and liner
looking more
like war paint these days,
preparing for battle.
But remember,
the most courageous warriors
are the ones
that show up unarmed,
yet ready
to defend their truths
by living them.

The Pink Temple

She glided into the room
in her pink glittery heels,
while the rest of us were beige.
She was met with some cackling,
other's questioning,
and a few,
admiring the color of innocence
juxtaposed with the style
of heightened power,
a commingling of feminine and masculine
that catches everyone's attention,
though only a few can carry off.

We all step into
our own place of worship
to fully embody
who we truly are.

Messengers of Grace at the Supermarket

I heard her
before I saw her,
sobbing in front
of the lined peanut butter jars
in aisle 3.

In the past,
I may have walked
past her awkwardly
as the other customers
were doing.
But today,
I chose to not look away
and broke the ice
with a stupid joke
that actually worked,
warm raindrops of laughter
mixing in
with the precipitation
of her icy tears.

Her mother had passed away,
suddenly,
unexpectedly,
just a mere few weeks ago
and she habitually
was about to grab
her Mom's favorite
off the shelf
when the reality
of her new normal
stung her into omission.

We stood there
for a few minutes
talking about peanut butter,
Moms, and grief
and how we brace ourselves
for anniversaries and birthdays,
but the simple, innocuous intricacies
that intertwine
to become the fabric of our lives
can also have grief
barreling through life's door.

I let her decide
when the conversation was over
and I wished her well
as she moved her shopping cart
to safer ground,
and me
into new territory,
happy I answered
the call of the wild.

Arboreal

The wisdom of the mighty Oak.
The timelessness of the Evergreen.
The smell of Eucalyptus.
The playfulness of a Palm.
The deep connections of an Aspen.
The productivity of a Maple.
The artistic expression of a Bonsai.
The empathy of a Weeping Willow.
The higher perspective of the Redwood.
The strength of Bamboo.
Even with their differences,
they all remain grounded and rooted,
while simultaneously
reaching for the stars.
Kinda like us.

Flowering

She picks me and
makes a wish,
her gentle secret
blown into existence,
but then again,
she always saw me differently
than everyone else.

So tired of being plain and ordinary,
an eyesore,
a weed,
undervalued and unwanted,
known only as stubborn and strong willed,
most try to destroy me
to prevent my presence
from being spread throughout.
Yet, she sees only the beauty in me,
like little suns scattered about,
thriving in the most difficult conditions,
never giving up.

She knows the divine winds
will carry her seeded dreams
great distances,
find a new resting place,
take root and fleurish.
I don't know her name,
but she must be called a dandelion
like me.

EPILOGUE

Heaven on Earth
tastes like chocolate,
smells like oranges,
sounds like laughter,
feels like satin,
and looks like you.

ACKNOWLEDGEMENTS

Though my books are more of an invitation than a dedication, I'd be remiss if I didn't thank a few special people who greatly assisted me with this book and those who have helped support, guide, and shape the launch of my business venture Burst & Fleurish, LLC.

Suzanne Verba-Hopkins
Michelle Arpin Begina
Sherri Novak
Mitch Rosacker

To my family, the poem *Summers in the Catskills* is devoted to you, as the memories of those times sustain me through today.

And to my daughter Mia, never measure my love for you based on the number of hours spent together, but the time that flies by when we do. By trying to be better for you, you make me a better me, and a forever us.

ABOUT THE AUTHOR

Michelle Kaplan has worked in Corporate America for over thirty years as a Human Resources professional with a focus on Organizational Effectiveness and Leadership Development. Her vision is to transform teams and corporate cultures by allowing individuals to collectively bring their true selves to work every day in the form of their unique talents and strengths. Whether strategizing and implementing organizational initiatives, coaching, or training, Michelle is passionate about motivating and empowering people into right action to live their soul's purpose. Her mission is to help those she works with reconnect with their personal power to create the outward changes they seek from within.

Since her breast cancer diagnosis in 2004, Michelle has been "walking the talk" by consciously aligning who she is with what she does. With her alarm set for early mornings most days, Michelle practices her unorthodox method of meditation, disguised in her early morning workouts, and poetry writing, with the intention of self-discovery, for at least an hour a day.

Her personal story of adopting her daughter from Guatemala was highlighted in Jack Canfield's book, *Living the Success Principles.* Michelle's personal and professional experiences, combined with her natural intuitiveness, provide a uniquely contemporary and relevant perspective throughout her writings on subjects about who we really are that have been explored for centuries.

Speaking loud, fast, and often, no one's more pleasantly surprised than Michelle that her unvarnished musings are organically chronicled in poetic verse. As a writer of fewer words, her natural writing style matches her personal mantra, "Keep it simple. Keep it real." Truth asks for only that.

For more about Michelle, visit her website:

www.BurstandFleurish.com

Poetry, experiences, and things for self-discovery